NEVER EVER

GIVE UP

the story of Bumper the dog

Written by Karen J. Roberts

Inspired by Bumper

CreateSpace, North Charleson, SC

"Love and compassion are necessities, not luxuries. Without them humanity cannot survive."
—Dalai Lama

"We are each made for goodness, love and compassion. Our lives are transformed as much as the world is when we live with these truths."
—Desmond Tutu

Introduction

This is the story of Bumper the Chow, and how she never, ever, ever gave up.

If ever there was a dog in need of a chance, it was Bumper. She needed someone to believe in her, to value her and to love her with all her imperfections. After all, isn't that what we all want out of life?

You see, Bumper was once a happy, healthy, bouncing, fluffy puppy! And everyone loves puppies. If you know anything about Chows, it's that they are one of the fluffiest dogs around!

So, Bumper began her life as a super fluffy puppy without a care in the world. She did all the normal puppy activities:

- *she played,*
- *she ate,*
- *she chewed on bones,*
- *she learned to have nice manners...*

Soon, she grew from a small, fluffy puppy into a big, fluffy dog. She was part of a family, which is what all dogs want. But sadly, our story doesn't end there. Like all dogs, Bumper grew older and started to slow down.

She couldn't get around as well anymore. Running and playing took a backseat to resting and lounging. She was still fluffy and lovable, but sadly, her medical bills were getting to be too expensive and her humans were neglecting to care for her properly. If you know anything about humans, you know they can sometimes make bad decisions. Bumper's humans were no exception.

Bumper was abandoned just when she was most in need of love. But don't feel sorry for Bumper. Bumper wouldn't want that. She would want you to think of her with all the joy and love in your heart.

Because this is the story of Bumper the Chow, and how she never, ever, ever gave up.

Poor old Bumper was down on her luck. She had once had a home, but now she wandered the cold, hard, frozen winter streets of **New York City** on her own. She was a stray dog, recently abandoned by her owners.

Even though her family gave up on her,
Bumper never gave up on herself.

Bumper's ears were very sore. Both of them were swollen and infected. She shook her head, and scratched them with her back legs the best she could, but her back legs weren't working so well either. She wasn't sure when her legs became so shaky. They used to carry her around just fine. She could run and jump and play. Now, however, she moved very slowly. Sometimes she even had trouble just standing up. She was determined to stand, though, so she could keep moving.

Bumper had some cuts and sores on her body that were painful, but because her ears were so itchy and bothersome, she stopped fussing with the cuts. It was hard for her to reach the sores with her tongue. She wanted to lick them to help them heal, but it seemed her old bones and muscles wouldn't quite cooperate anymore.

The sneezing and itching in her nose and throat had gotten unbearable. She tried to forget about all the painful issues with her health, but it wasn't easy. Curling up to sleep was no longer comfortable. Every time she settled in to rest she had to scratch, and itch, and sneeze and reposition herself. Even with the pain, she was happy to be alive, and she knew she couldn't give up.

This is when Bumper learned the meaning of the word

"courage."

When Bumper's eyes became runny and sore, she did her best to rub them with her paws to try to ease the pain. She really needed a bath, however, and so the dirt from her paws and fur irritated her eyes even more.

You could say that Bumper was a bit of a mess.
It wasn't her fault, though.

Bumper knew that most humans try to avoid seeing something sad. She knew it was human nature for some people to pretend not to see the pain and suffering of others simply to protect their own heart. That's why she was so grateful to the people who saved her.

When Bumper was finally brought in to Animal Control she needed a miracle. The smells and sounds of the place made her feel worried. She waited for a veterinarian to look in her itchy ears and hoped for soothing drops in her painful eyes, but sadly, no help came. There was no medicine, no eye drops, and no vet. Even though her condition made the humans at Animal Control give up on her, Bumper never gave up on herself.

Curious and hopeful, Bumper looked into the eyes of a kind human from the **Pet Adoption League of New York, Inc.** tilted her tired head and asked for help.

"Please take a chance on me," she thought,
"I'm worth it, I promise."

This is when Bumper learned
the meaning of the word
"rescue."

This kind human took Bumper to a vet to get her help. She whined and "ouched" her way through the stops and starts of the car ride. Each bump in the road reminded her of why she needed help. With each minute that passed, Bumper was more and more grateful to be off the streets and out of Animal Control.

"See!" she thought. "Things are looking up!"

Finally, she got to see a vet. Although it was unpleasant to be examined while she was so sick, she was relieved to get some help.

After her visit at the vet was over, she wondered where she would be going next. It turns out she was going on a vacation! Bumper would take a trip from New York to Cape Cod, Massachusetts! Bumper felt like the luckiest dog in the world.

Even though her ears, nose and throat were itchy, her eyes sore, her legs wobbly and her cuts painful, she felt happy for a chance to take a trip.

Through all her challenges,
she found a way to wag her tail
and feel excited about her adventures.

The medicine from the vet was starting to work. She relaxed in the backseat and watched the world go by. Bumper was optimistic that wherever she ended up, she would find a way to feel better again.

When Bumper arrived at her new vacation home in beautiful Cape Cod, two new loving humans greeted her. Their kindness was real. They welcomed Bumper into their home and looked past her imperfections. They saw her smile and her heart. **She felt their love and acceptance.**

**This is when Bumper learned
the meaning of the word**

"compassion."

A new chapter in Bumper's life was about to begin! She had survived being abandoned by her family. She had survived, lonely and sick, on the cold city streets by herself. She had survived Animal Control and had made it out of the building alive, even in her terrible condition. And finally, she had survived the transition to her new life.

**This is when Bumper learned
the meaning of the word
"triumph."**

Bumper's new foster parents, Tracey and Denis, were devoted to getting her healthy and giving her the best life possible.

Bumper had warm, soapy baths to keep her fur coat beautiful and fluffy. This made her feel happy, comfortable and loved. Her ears, nose, throat, eyes and the cuts on her skin had all healed, and she was no longer itchy and uncomfortable.

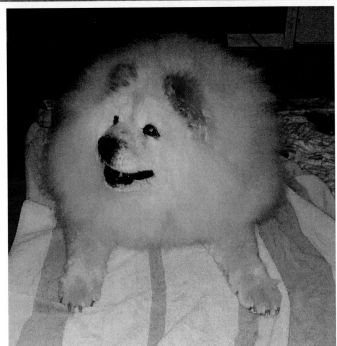

Bumper still, however, had trouble getting around on her wobbly legs. Getting up was a struggle and walking was almost too painful to bear. Tracey and Denis went to great lengths to give Bumper every opportunity for a wonderful life.

She had to take a lot of medications, but luckily for Tracey and Denis, Bumper loved to eat so they could skillfully hide Bumper's pills in her food. They cooked her gourmet meals with love and care and fed her as if she were the Queen of England! Even though she had trouble walking, she still managed sometimes to make it to the kitchen at mealtime. Usually, though, Bumper preferred to have her meals hand-delivered to her bedside. This was the life!

Bumper's favorite foods were chicken, steak, sweet potatoes, turkey, meatballs and gluten-free pasta. Her most favorite meal, though, was teriyaki beef. What a treat that was for Bumper!

Having a full belly, clean fur, and a loving family made Bumper happy. At 13 years old, she had a lot of health challenges. So, she decided to live in the moment and make each day special. She never thought about her time as a lonely, sick stray on the cold streets of New York. She forgot all about her past troubles. She didn't think about the future, because it was uncertain what tomorrow would bring. She made the most of each day with a joyous and grateful heart, living in each glorious moment as a spoiled and loved pet.

**This is when Bumper learned
the meaning of the word**

"gratitude."

Because Tracey and Denis were so devoted to her care, Bumper was taken to physical therapy to help her walk. She got to roll on a giant ball to help her stretch her sore legs. Bumper loved the attention and thought it was all a big game.

She had so much fun she would smile with delight!

Bumper even had hydrotherapy. She loved it! Walking and swimming in the water helped her regain strength in her sore muscles and provided much-needed rehabilitation for Bumper's legs. She was very proud of her swimming skills and looked forward to showing off her doggie paddle.

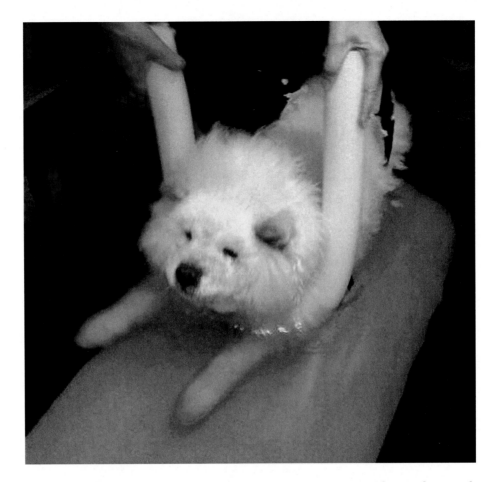

I think it's safe to say that everyone at the dog therapy center fell in love with Bumper!

Bumper's favorite activity was going out on the town to greet her many new fans and to make new friends. Since it was difficult for her to get around, Bumper had her very own *Radio Flyer* red wagon to ride in. She felt so special in her wagon and her joy was contagious.

She proudly smiled at everyone she met along the way.
Every day Bumper rode in her wagon to the park, beaches
and downtown. She looked like a big, fluffy marshmallow.
People would flock to her side to pet her and see her bright
and happy smile.

I think it's safe to say that everyone fell in love with Bumper!

Some days she got to go for a ride in the car, which was a special treat for her. Denis made a bed for her in the front seat so she could see out the window and smell the fresh air. She was the perfect co-pilot.

Going on outings, keeping up with her fans and spending time at doggie therapy to stay healthy could be tiring, too. It's a good thing Bumper was an excellent lounger. After all, this was her vacation, and it's important to relax and enjoy life when you are on vacation.

Bumper enjoyed sunning herself on the deck, but if it was too sunny, she preferred the shade under her umbrella. And, if it was too hot, she welcomed a gentle breeze from the electric fan provided by Tracey and Denis.

When she had had enough of the outdoors, she had many comfy choices inside, as well. There were dog beds, couches and plenty of blankets. Denis happily carried Bumper to her favorite spots in the yard, deck and inside the house whenever her legs were too weak to get around.

This is when Bumper learned the meaning of the word

"diva."

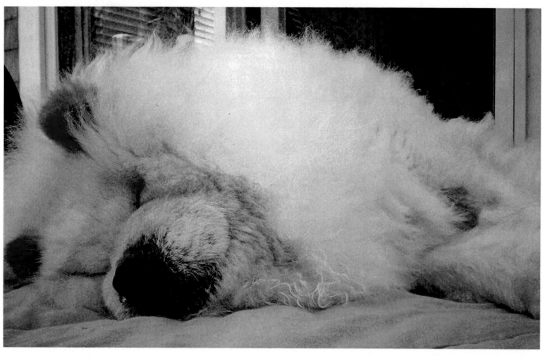

Bumper's favorite part about her Cape Cod vacation was all her four-legged friends! She had been so lonely when she was living on the streets, and now she always had several foster siblings to keep her company.

Bumper's foster siblings were all rescues, living the good life with Tracey and Denis. They were all grateful to be given a second chance, and they loved spending time together.

They guarded the house, sauntered through the neighborhood, and did their best sloth impressions in the sun. There was always plenty of food, treats, toys and beds to go around. **What more could any dog ask for?.**

Bumper's life with Tracey and Denis was full of love. They provided her with a routine she could count on that made her feel safe. She spread joy and happiness to everyone she met. Her fluffy coat and smiling face made the world a better place.

But Bumper was an old gal, and as much as she loved her life, she knew it wouldn't last forever. Soon the angels called for her. It was her time to go, and Bumper was at peace. She left her loving humans behind with a grateful heart, and now she runs free with no more pain.

But don't feel sad for Bumper. Bumper wouldn't want that. She would want you to be happy for the life she had. She would always be grateful for the second chance she was given and for the kind people who took a chance on a senior dog when she needed it most. Bumper never gave up on herself, and thankfully her compassionate rescuers didn't either.

Bumper's only wish is to show the world that every dog matters. Bumper would want her story to inspire other humans to open their hearts and homes to shelter pets. She would want everyone to realize that just because a dog is old, or not feeling well, or having trouble getting around, doesn't mean they don't deserve a chance. We all need a miracle at some point in our lives. We all need someone to take a chance on us.

Be that person to an animal in need.
Your heart will **grow**, your life will be rich with love,
and **you will never regret being kind.**

Don't feel bad for Bumper. Remember her will to survive, her joyful spirit and her precious life that was so worth saving. Use the special feeling Bumper's story brought to your heart by paying it forward to another dog in need.

This is when Bumper hopes you learn the meaning of the words

"rescue," "foster," "adopt," and "love."

The End.

12 Alarming Facts About Pet Homelessness in the U.S.

Let's dig in to some of the cold, hard facts on pet homelessness, shall we?

1 There are about 70 million stray animals living in the U.S.

2 Of this 70 million, only about six to eight million cats and dogs enter the nation's 3,500 shelters every year, according to the Humane Society of the United States.

3 That evens out to about five homeless animals for every homeless person in the U.S, reports DoSomething.org.

4 Out of six to eight million cats and dogs, one in four animals brought into shelters are pit bulls or pit-associated breeds and mixes – currently the most (wrongly) marginalized dogs in the U.S. and many other parts of the world.

5 The two main reasons animals end up in shelters are because they've either been surrendered by their guardians or picked up off the street by animal control officers.

6 Around 10 percent of animals entering shelters have been spayed or neutered, which is problematic considering in just six years, one un-spayed female dog and her offspring can create 67,000 dogs and one un-spayed female cat and her offspring can produce 420,000 kittens in seven years, reports Watatuga Humane Society.

7 About 30 percent of shelter dogs are eventually reclaimed by their guardians, with cats far behind at only 2 to 5 percent.

8 What's more, only about three to four million cats and dogs are adopted from shelters each year.

9 Know what this means? Nearly half of all animals that arrive in U.S. shelters are euthanized because there is a lack of space and adopters, amounting to roughly 2.7 million dead animals every year or five out of every ten dogs and seven out of every ten cats – that's like 80,000 animals per week.

10 Five out of every ten shelter dogs each year amounts to about 5,500 euthanized dogs every day.

11 Of all the dogs that enter the shelter system, pit bull types have it the worst with a shockingly high euthanasia rate of 93 percent.

12 To pay for all of this – the impoundment, sheltering, euthanasia and subsequent disposal of homeless animals – U.S. taxpayers shell out between one to two billion dollars annually.

What this fact breakdown ultimately reveals is that:
(1) breeding animals for the sake of profit or simply because someone "wants" a certain type of dog is highly unnecessary and unsustainable – there are clearly plenty of dogs and cats awaiting homes — and

(2) that the power to change these statistics is in our hands.

We can say no to pet stores and "pet for sale" ads and instead chose adoption as the one and only route to take. We can spay and neuter our adopted companion animals to ensure that they will not contribute to the influx of animals in shelters (check out Spay USA for low-cost spay/neuter clinics in your area).

We can also enact change at all levels of our society from the local level (no kill, spay and neuter, and trap-neuter-release programs, anyone?) all the way up to the state and national level by calling on our elected officials to hold irresponsible pet guardians and pet breeders accountable and to put measures into place that would phase in the choice of shelter and rescue adoption over pet purchase, like Pheonix, Ariz. recently did by banning the sale of dogs and cats in pet stores.

We can make sure that no cat or dog becomes a heartbreaking statistic ever again – we need only step up to the plate and never back down.

These pet homelessness statistics and information
were obtained from onegreenplanet.org

Open your heart and home
to a shelter pet.
Thanks for caring!

Caryl Shulman with her dogs, Angie and Clancy.

For updates on our rescue efforts, please like our Facebook pages:
Pet Adoption League of NY - Chow Chow Rescue,
and
Bumper's Legacy.

About Pet Adoption League of New York, Inc.

Pet Adoption League of New York, Inc. (PALofNY) is a 501C3 rescue organization devoted to saving "at risk" dogs in kill shelters around the US. The President, Caryl Shulman, has been involved in rescue for over 40 years and incorporated PALofNY in 2001. Caryl's fondness for chows stems from the fact that her parents had chows before she was born and she grew up with them. She and her husband have had over 15 chows as family members. Two more share their home at the present time.

PALofNY is a member of the Mayor's Alliance for NYC animals, and a New Hope Partner. PALofNY is a recognized and well respected chow rescue organization and its President is a member of the Chow Welfare Committee of the National Chow Chow Breed Club. PALofNY is also a Network Partner of the Best Friends Animal Society. PALofNY is well known for its rescue of dogs with medical and behavioral issues as well as unwanted senior and abandoned dogs like Bumper. Caryl would like to thank everyone involved in Bumper's rescue and all the volunteers for Pet Adoption League of New York, Inc. who have made our rescue organization the success it is.

To contact the rescue by email, you can reach us at PALofNY@yahoo.com or PALofNY501c3@gmail.com

About Tracey and Denis, Bumper's Foster Parents

Tracey and Denis have been fostering dogs since 2009. In their six years as loving caregivers to animals in need, they have fostered 55 dogs, six of which they eventually adopted.

Although they primarily foster for PAL of NY, Inc. they do occasionally foster for other rescues that share the same values and ethics. According to Tracey, her foster situation changes every day. Their flexibility as foster parents allows them to assist with overnight stays for dogs in the middle of their transport to their final destination. Stepping in for short term fostering, as well as caring for long term, "at risk" dogs like Bumper, exemplifies the compassion and selflessness crucial to operating a successful animal rescue organization like PAL of NY, Inc.

"A special Thank You to Tracey and Denis Sparagis for the incredible work they do in rehabilitating "At Risk" rescue dogs. These precious souls would never survive as long as they do without the dedication and love Tracey and Denis provide."

-Caryl Shulman
President, Pet Adoption League of New York, Inc.

The History of the Chow Chow

Scientific research indicates that the chow chow originated in China over 3,000 years ago. Because of their intelligence, loyalty and bravery they were the dogs used by the Manchurian Emperor's guards to patrol the palace grounds and protect the family from marauding mountain lions. Chinese statues referred to as a FU dogs, date back over 3000 years. They are believed to be representations of the chow chow.

In the early 1800's, Queen Victoria's sailors brought back several chows from China. They became popular in England and the Queen had several chows. The first chow was exhibited in the US in 1890. The breed became popular in the US starting in the early 1900's.

The Chow Chow is by nature, a very loyal, regal dog. He is very intelligent with a calm disposition. He is fiercely devoted to his family, especially the children, and is content to lie quietly in their presence, not requiring a lot of exercise. Because of his protective nature, it's important that the chow be constantly socialized with other people and dogs outside the family so that he can be an active participant in his family's lives.

DOGS COME INTO OUR LIVES TO
TEACH US ABOUT LOVE.

THEY DEPART TO
TEACH US ABOUT LOSS.

A NEW DOG NEVER REPLACES
AN OLD DOG,
IT MERELY EXPANDS THE HEART.

About the Author

Karen J. Roberts has her BA degree in English from Syracuse University and has spent her professional career in Healthcare Information Technology. An avid animal lover and pet owner her whole life, her true passion is animal advocacy. As a writer, humane educator, animal rescue volunteer, animal rights advocate, and vegan, Karen feels a deep connection to a cruelty-free lifestyle and believes each of us can make choices that contribute to a more compassionate world for all living creatures. Her goal is to inspire leadership and advocacy in the younger generations.

She shares her peaceful life in Wellington, Florida
with her six dogs and one cat.
To learn more about Karen and her books, visit
www.thelittlebluedog.com

Other titles by Karen J. Roberts
The Little Blue Dog
The Little Blue Dog Has a Birthday Party
The Little Blue Dog Goes to School
Too Many Dogs
Homeward Hounds
The Gentle Beagle
A Terrier's Tale
Peanut Butter & Pumpernickel
Super Mom!
The Lollipop Garden

Karen and her rescued Rat Terrier named Tucker.
Tucker was a stray dog at the county shelter. After 45 days he was out of time
and listed as URGENT. During a visit to the shelter, Karen fell in love with his
sweet face and saved his life. He visits Elementary School children teaching
them about animal kindness. Tucker is the inspiration for Karen's book
"A Terrier's Tale."

Photo by Melissa McDaniel

Author Karen J. Roberts happily volunteered her time to write
Never Ever Give Up, The story of Bumper the dog after meeting
Caryl Shulman and hearing about Bumper's rescue.

100% of the proceeds from the sale of the book are donated to
PALofNY Inc. for their continued rescue efforts.

Courage: the quality of mind or spirit that enables a person to face difficulty, danger, pain. Without fear; bravery.

Rescue: to free or deliver from confinement, violence, danger, or evil.

Compassion: a feeling of deep sympathy and sorrow for another who is stricken by misfortune, accompanied by a strong desire to alleviate the suffering.

Triumph: a significant success or noteworthy achievement; instance or occasion of victory.

Gratitude: the quality or feeling of being grateful or thankful.

Diva: a famous and successful woman who is very attractive and fashionable.

Foster: to promote the growth or development of; further; encourage. to care for or cherish.

Adopt: to choose or take as one's own; make one's own by selection or assent. To take and rear as one's own, specifically by a formal legal act.

Love: a profoundly tender, passionate affection for another person. A feeling of warm personal attachment or deep affection.

Made in the USA
San Bernardino, CA
07 September 2017